CONTENTS

ZAIRE, GABON, AND THE CONGO

BY GERALD NEWMAN

FRANKLIN WATTS
New York | London | Toronto | Sydney | 1981
A FIRST BOOK

FOR ROSEANN
and good old Tessie

The author would like to thank
Mona Bregman, Mary Cullen,
Michelle Epstein, Geri Feldman,
Shelley Hendlin, Steven Storman,
and John Van Axen
for their assistance in
the preparation of this book.

Cover design by Jackie Schuman

Photographs courtesy of:
Photo Researchers (Christa Armstrong): p. 19;
Photo Researchers (Georg Gerster): pp. 29, 38;
Tass from Sovfoto: p. 40; Eastfoto: pp. 50, 54.

Maps courtesy of Vantage Art, Inc.

Library of Congress Cataloging in Publication Data

Newman, Gerald.
Zaire, Gabon, and the Congo.

(A First book)
Bibliography: p.
Includes index.
SUMMARY: An introduction to three countries
of Equatorial Africa, once known for their dense
rain forests and now, due to their mineral wealth,
increasingly important in the world industrial
community.
1. Zaire—Juvenile literature. 2. Gabon—
Juvenile literature. 3. Congo (Brazzaville)—
Juvenile literature. [1. Zaire. 2. Gabon.
3. Congo (Brazzaville)] I. Title.
DT644.N48   967.5'1   80-25245
ISBN 0-531-04279-0

ZAIRE, GABON, AND THE CONGO

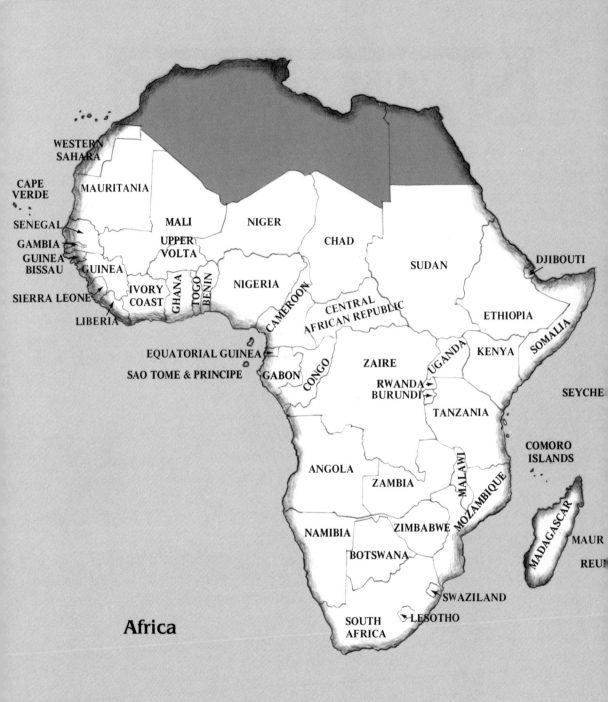

Africa

THE HISTORY OF THE EQUATORIAL COUNTRIES

The equator runs practically through the center of Gabon, the Congo, and Zaire. That is why these countries are often referred to as Equatorial Africa. They are also known as the rain forest countries because so much of their land is covered by dense, wet forestland. Because of this tropical location, for many years, they have been Africa's mystery nations, lands explored by the few who dared to intrude on the hot, wet climate, the curious tribes, the savage animals, and the slave traders.

Even today, though slave traders are long gone and industry is beginning to flourish, these countries continue to be centers of the unusual—lands of extremes—nations where one can see the present, the future, and the past, existing around the bend from each other.

Hunters still use spears and nets. Yet, the uranium for the first atom bomb came from this region. Diamonds are dug from the earth by people who wear leopards' teeth around their necks. Modern hotel rooms are air-conditioned, yet witch doctors still attempt to cure illnesses and remove curses. Handmade dugout log canoes float down the river from straw hut villages to modern jetports.

A look at these interesting nations will show why they are so exciting, so unusual, and so important.

Eager to find a route to the wealth of India, Portugal, in the fifteenth century, began sending sailing expeditions around the coast of Africa. It was on one of these journeys that explorers first ventured into the dark, mysterious continent.

In 1482, a Portuguese naval captain, Diogo Cao, discovered the mouth of the Congo River. It was here that he found the Bakongo, a Bantu-speaking people whose territory spread from northern Angola along both banks of the Congo River, to the Atlantic, and to the Kwango River in present-day Zaire.

Cao was in search of the ManiKongo, the chief who bound together many small tribes into a mighty kingdom. Cao believed if he followed the river, he would find the African ruler. But the trip up the river was too treacherous and Cao was forced to turn back. In about 1488, Cao disappeared without a trace.

In March 1491, Duarte Lopes, another Portuguese explorer, finally met the ManiKongo and succeeded in converting him, his wife, his eldest son, and thousands of natives to Christianity. But the Christian missionaries' cruel treatment of the natives caused a revolt and the spread of Christianity was soon halted. Moreover, many missionaries who had claimed large tracts of land to live on took slaves to work their plantations.

Slave-trading soon grew into a huge profit-making venture. In time, England, Holland, Spain, and France entered into competition with Portugal. They, too, were eager to reap the profits from ivory, ebony, and slaves, and managed to do so better than the Portuguese. In fact, by 1789, France had seventy companies trading on the African coast. Portugal's power was virtually eliminated.

FRANCE IN GABON

Spurred on by the word "equality," as part of the slogan of the French Revolution: "liberty, equality, and fraternity," France condemned slavery in 1793. But Napoleon quickly reinstated it. It was not until 1848, that France finally abolished slavery. The following year, with fifty-three slaves released as "freemen" from a Senegal-bound slaveship, they established Libreville (in Gabon) as a freedom town, the only port along Africa's west coast that was not a slave-trading depot. However, it took forty more years before the abolition of slavery took total effect in Equatorial Africa.

By 1841, the French had signed treaties establishing themselves at the mouth of the Como River. While patrolling the coastal waters in search of slave ships, they discovered Gabon's wealth of ivory, ebony, sandalwood, wax, gum, and rubber. This discovery prompted additional treaties with many native kings so that the tradespeople could export these natural treasures to France.

Along with the traders and the military, came the missionaries who built missions, churches, and schools. And with the missionaries came more treaties for more land down the coast. The only territory not explored and exploited were the dense rain forests of the interior.

INTO THE INTERIOR

By the end of the 1850s, curiosity about what could be found in that territory grew strong and it began to be explored further. In 1876, a Frenchman, Pierre Savorgnan de Brazza, accompanied by a team of scientists and naturalists, ventured into the interior.

The following year, de Brazza founded Franceville and Brazzaville, in what is today the Republic of the Congo. He set up outposts and entered into treaties with African chiefs. One of the treaties was with the Bateke king, the Mokako. Signed in 1880, it joined a number of loosely knit tribes under the protection of France. Once ratified on November 20, 1882, it united what is today Gabon and the People's Republic of the Congo, into the French Republic.

Under French rule, the coastal tribes in Gabon and the Republic of the Congo continued to flourish. Commerce and "Europeanization" spread into the interior through trade agreements with the English and the Germans. Missionaries set up more churches and schools, and large commercial companies divided up the land for exploration and trade purposes.

In 1886, de Brazza became commissioner general of the Congo and Noel Ballay was appointed lieutenant governor of Gabon. The area was now officially two separate colonies. Two years later, both colonies were united under the name the French Congo. Libreville was designated the capital.

Meanwhile, Henry M. Stanley, an American newspaper reporter who had originally set out to find the missing missionary, David Livingstone, continued Livingstone's quest to follow the Lualaba River to the Atlantic Ocean.

Stanley founded the capital city of Vivi, and set up a trading station which he called Leopoldville, for King Leopold of Belgium who financed his trip through loans from bankers. Leopoldville is now called Kinshasa.

In 1884, King Leopold claimed the rights to the land for himself, not for Belgium. The king called the land the Congo Free State. The following year, the General Act of Berlin, a document signed by fourteen major world powers, insured that the Congo basin would be free for trade and exploration to all nations, and open to missionaries of all religions. It was further decided that the basin would be neutral territory during war, that slavery would remain abolished, and that the living conditions of its population would be improved.

THE CONGO FREE STATE

However, the document did not include one important point. King Leopold had created the International African Association which now controlled over 1,000,000 square miles (2,600,000 sq km) of the Congo basin. All land, ivory, and rubber now belonged to him. And if he so decided, a village could be destroyed if it did not meet the quota of rubber and ivory it was required to extract. Instead of having Europeans accused of mistreating the natives, other Africans (often cannibals) were retained to administer the punishment. The result was the reduction of the population from about twenty million to nine million within fifteen years.

Of course, this treatment was kept secret from the world. Officials were paid off and missionaries were kept silent because of Leopold's deep "religious convictions." If someone threatened to expose the true conditions, that person either was paid to keep silent or mysteriously disappeared.

In 1890, the Congo was not earning enough money for Leopold. In order to increase his profits, Leopold mortgaged a large part of the Congo to a banker. When he was unable to repay the banker, Leopold decided to give the land to Belgium. But Belgium did not want the burden of supporting a poor financial investment.

Later, when the exporting of rubber and ivory changed the financial condition of the Congo for the better, Belgium demanded that the land be annexed to them. In 1907, Leopold sold the valuable Congo Free State to Belgium.

By November 14, 1908, the Congo Free State had become the Belgian Congo. A new charter was drawn up stating how the territory would be governed. But Belgium was really concerned more with profit-making than with colonization. Tribal chieftans were often held hostage if local workers didn't meet their quotas of ivory and rubber. Treated with disrespect, they now strutted around in European top hats instead of the lush brocades and velvets they once wore. A way of life had been totally destroyed and so had a people's dignity.

World War I brought new demands for rubber to be shipped to Europe. By improving labor conditions and by eliminating quotas, men were now encouraged to work under contract. Railroads were built to transport copper, diamonds, and agricultural products. Farming and fertilization were taught and farming settlements were established.

FRENCH EQUATORIAL AFRICA

In the meantime, on January 15, 1910, Gabon, Chad, the Central African Republic (then called Ubangi), and the Congo were united and given the name of French Equatorial Africa. France believed that uniting these colonies would simplify their administration and would cut costs. Brazzaville became the capital and Libreville was reduced to the chief town of Gabon. Libreville's economic stability fell.

Excessive hard labor, the sending of thousands of the strongest men to build railroads, rampant disease, starvation, and the shipping of 680,000 able-bodied Africans to fight in

World War I, destroyed the manpower and depleted the population of the country.

WORLD WAR II

Again in World War II, men from Equatorial Africa were mobilized and shipped to Europe as members of the French military. The Congo had been placed under the authority of General Charles de Gaulle, but Gabon remained under the rule of the Vichy government—which was against de Gaulle.

The 1944 Brazzaville Conference decreed that France's colonies would be represented in the Assembly of the New French Republic. However, at the elections of 1945, only one representative to the Assembly was permitted and he represented *all* of France's African territories. More important, no mention was ever made of the Congo's chance for self-government.

Finally, later that year, each territory in French Equatorial Africa was granted its own representative. The new French constitution granted equal rights to all of France's territories and allowed them to choose their own relationship to the mother country—from total dependence on France, to near independence. The constitution also allowed money to be invested for the promotion of social and economic development of its territories. However, it did not give Africans who became French citizens the right to vote. In the long run, African representation was inadequate. It had no influence and no power to object to anything it believed hampered its progress. The Africans would have been satisfied had these reforms taken place twenty-five years earlier. But now, they found their way of life totally unacceptable.

India, Indochina, Morocco, and Tunisia had become independent. Algeria was fighting France at that very moment. There was every reason for Gabon to become independent, too. Moreover, the United Nations was welcoming the freedom of nations throughout the world.

TOWARD INDEPENDENCE
IN GABON

In 1956, a law was drafted that allowed each territory to elect a Government Council. It gave all people the right to vote, and best of all, it established self-rule for the territory.

On September 28, 1958, de Gaulle created the French Community, a union of France and all its territories. Its constitution granted self-rule to all French colonies, and the new Republic of Gabon was officially proclaimed on November 29, 1958. Now the Gabonese could rule themselves, even though Gabon was not yet totally independent.

After Gabon's own constitution was ratified on February 19, 1959, Leon M'Ba became the prime minister. In 1960, the constitution of the French Community was amended so that France's self-ruled states could become independent and still remain members of the community. Finally, on August 17, 1960, complete independence was achieved. A month later, Gabon was admitted to the United Nations. M'Ba was elected President of the Republic on February 12, 1961. He died in office in 1967.

M'Ba was succeeded by his Vice-President, Albert-Bernard Bongo—a man considered by the Gabonese to be strong and clear-thinking. He immediately initiated the "renovation" of Gabon.

Bongo began by allowing France even greater participation in Gabon's development than during the colonial period. He has allowed the French to run new businesses, schools, and

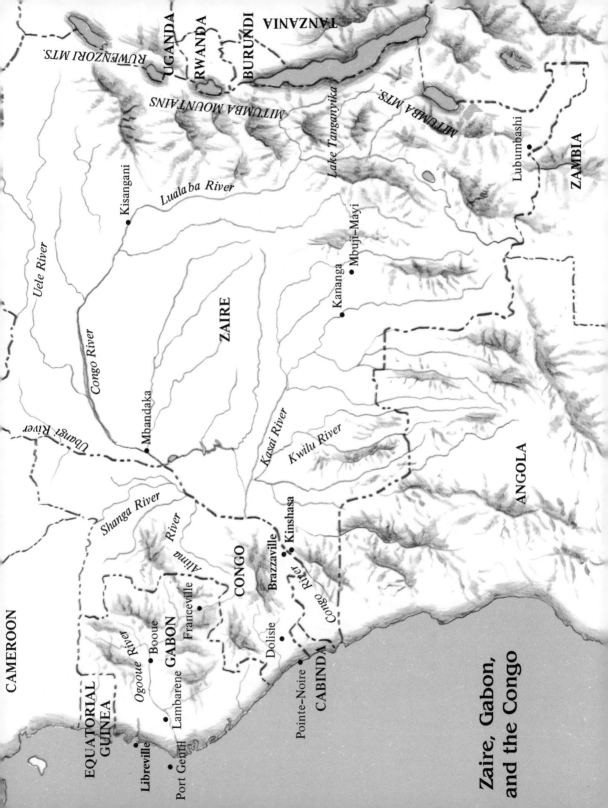

Zaire, Gabon, and the Congo

CAMEROON

EQUATORIAL GUINEA

GABON

CONGO

CABINDA

ANGOLA

ZAIRE

ZAMBIA

TANZANIA

BURUNDI

RWANDA

UGANDA

RUWENZORI MTS.

MITUMBA MOUNTAINS

MITUMBA MTS.

Lake Tanganyika

Libreville

Port Gentil

Lambarene

Boue

Franceville

Dolisie

Pointe-Noire

Brazzaville

Kinshasa

Mbandaka

Kisangani

Kananga

Mbuji-Mayi

Lubumbashi

Uele River

Congo River

Ubangi River

Shanga River

Ogooue River

Alima River

Kasai River

Kwilu River

Luala ba River

Congo River

banks, and to serve him as advisers. Though the lumber, oil, and mining industries provide the major financial strength of Gabon, Bongo's prime goal is to increase his country's agricultural and livestock growth so that he can eliminate the need to import food for his people. If he is successful, the combination of reduced imports and greater exports of natural resources will raise Gabon's economy and provide more schools, hospitals, hydroelectric power, transportation, and cultural centers for the Gabonese citizens.

Since his election in 1973, Bongo has already raised the per capita income of Gabon to the highest level in black Africa.

TOWARD INDEPENDENCE
IN ZAIRE

After World War II, groups united through tribal or religious beliefs banded together. By the 1950s, these groups, called *evolués,* became interested in the politics of the Congo and the place of black people in the running of the country.

Within two years, many political groups emerged throughout the country—so many, in fact, that it was impossible to create any unified strength.

As these groups gathered more power, the government began a gradual program leading to the Congo's independence. But the idea led to mistrust between the Belgians and the Africans. And rioting broke out between the rival Lulua and Luba peoples and soon spread to the major Congo cities.

In May 1960, elections were held for a new Parliament. Patrice Lumumba, an outspoken advocate of Congo independence, was elected prime minister and Joseph Kasavubu, President. Independence day was set for June 30. But it was not a joyful day. Tensions still ran high between the Africans and the Belgians, and between the different African tribes. After only five days, more rioting broke out. The army mutinied and public authority fell apart. Belgian troops were called in to evacuate Europeans.

On September 5, the government was placed into the hands of Joseph Mobutu, a tough, Israeli-trained national army commander.

But rebellions continued in the northern and eastern parts of the country. On August 5, Stanleyville was taken by rebels called the Simbas (Swahili for "lions"). In order to stop the Simbas, Belgian troops began, on November 24, to capture rebel-held cities. They parachuted into Stanleyville to evacuate hostages. The following day, Mobutu declared himself President for the next five years.

In 1965, Mobutu was officially elected President, a position he still holds. Assuming absolute power, he became known as the "Guide" or the "Founder-President." Only his picture is permitted to hang in public places. Mobutu's power is so strong that even the people's way of life is based on "Mobutism"—the President's writings and teachings. No longer is June 30 the official anniversary date of the country. It is now November 24, the date Mobutu claimed the presidency.

On October 27, 1971, he changed the name of the Democratic Republic of the Congo to the Republic of Zaire—a name based on the Portuguese mispronunciation of *Nzari,* a Bantu word for "river."

Until 1977, Zaire enjoyed relative peace. In March of that year, 4,000 Katangan rebels, based in Angola, captured the Shaba province. With Moroccan troops to help him, Mobutu's army overtook the rebels and the "eighty-day war" came to an end. On May 13, 1978, the Katangans again attacked. This time, their target was Kolwezi, the mining center. Though the attack was quickly overcome, the toll was heavy. There was considerable damage to the mines, an important source of Zairean income. A 2,500 man inter-African peacekeeping force was called for to maintain security. As of 1979, Kolwezi began to regain its strength. Angola and Zaire agreed to reestablish ties and reopen the railroad, so necessary to the economy of both countries. The peacekeeping force was withdrawn and workers have returned. A Belgium-trained army of Zaireans guards the city.

Mobutu's philosophy has been one of a strong nationalization of all of Zaire's industry and agriculture. He coined the phrase "Let's roll up our sleeves," and it is now the government's slogan. Known as the "prophet" and the "savior," Mobutu's name has often been substituted for God in Catholic hymns.

TOWARD INDEPENDENCE IN
THE REPUBLIC OF THE CONGO

Another important change occurred in 1956, but this time it was in the Republic of the Congo. Fulbert Youlou, a parish priest, started his political career. Beginning as mayor of Brazzaville, he organized his own political party, the UDDIA (the Democratic Union for the Protection of African Interests). His first motion was to make Brazzaville the capital. Rioting, provoked by rival party militants, broke out; the police were called in and the opposition party walked out in protest. Left with only his own party, he was immediately elected premier. That November, the National Assembly voted Youlou President of the Re-

[12]

public. When the Congo became fully independent on August 15, 1960, Youlou and his party were in total control.

He united all the political parties into one national party. Though Youlou's rule was basically pro-Western and pro-French, many citizens were unhappy with him. They felt that he was too tightly controlled by French President Charles de Gaulle. Labor unions called a general strike. When bargaining failed, Youlou resigned from office on August 15, 1963. The following day, an eight-member political government was appointed. Alphonse Massemba-Debat became President of the Republic.

The new government was less involved with France and more closely tied to other revolutionary African nations. The economy was under tighter government control and an alliance with Communist countries grew stronger.

In time, the government leaned toward a Communistic philosophy, angering the Catholics, about one third of the Congo population. As a result, many missionary priests were expelled from the Congo. All trade unions were dissolved and instead, a single government-controlled organization was formed.

Massemba-Debat resigned in 1968 for political reasons. In his place, Marien Ngouabi became the head of a military government, and on January 1, 1969, he became President.

During that year, Ngouabi tried to end ethnic conflicts. At the same time, he strengthened his own powers and moved toward encouraging greater foreign investments by private individuals. He also formed the Congolese Labor party (PCT), the Congo's only political party.

On January 1, 1970, the country was proclaimed the People's Republic of the Congo. Within three days, the government

[13]

resigned and the new Council of State, with Ngouabi as President of the Republic, was formed. In his oath of office, Ngouabi swore loyalty to the Congolese people, the revolution, the Labor party, and the principles of Communism.

From the outset, Ngouabi's term of office was problem-ridden. During the first three years, numerous attempts were made to overthrow the government and hundreds were sentenced to prison terms. Some were killed. The police force was disbanded and replaced by the People's Militia.

By 1975, the PCT was no longer satisfied with Ngouabi. It called his leadership weak, his association with the public ineffective, and his civil servants more self-serving than country-serving. On March 18, 1977, Ngouabi was assassinated. Within a week, a military committee headed by Colonel Joachim Yhombi-Opango, began to run the country. On April 15, 1977, Yhombi-Opango became President, only to resign in 1979. The current President is Colonel Denis Sassou-Ngouesso, who was appointed by the Congolese Worker's party.

Three undeveloped, hostile environments, born as vague mysterious entities, plagued by nature's cruelty and society's inhumanity, have become, in just over five hundred years, three self-governing, independent nations. Though they still suffer the pains of growth, the discomfort of their climate, the agony of economic woes, they have grown into three nations—Zaire, The Republic of the Congo, and Gabon—prepared to face tomorrow courageously, intelligently, and proudly.

2
ZAIRE AND ITS PEOPLE

Zaire is the third largest country in Africa with an area of 902,769 square miles (2,344,855 sq km). As of the 1977 census, its population was 26,300,000, making it the continent's fourth most populated country.

On its western border are the Zaire and Ubangi rivers, which separate it from the Republic of the Congo. On its other borders, it is surrounded by nine neighboring countries: the Central African Republic and the Sudan to the north; Uganda, Rwanda, Burundi, and Tanzania on the east; The Congo on the west; Zambia and Angola at the south. Its southern border at Angola stretches west to the Atlantic Ocean, providing it with a small western seacoast.

In the western and central parts of the country, the climate is hot, 68° F–86° F (20° C–30° C), and humid. In the eastern and southeastern portions, where the land is higher, 5,000–16,000 feet (1,524–4,877 m), and the humidity is lower, the temperature usually varies between 59° F and 68° F (15° C–20° C). The mountainous Kivu area on Zaire's east coast maintains a pleasant, Mediterranean-like climate throughout the year.

THE PEOPLE
AND THEIR LANGUAGES

Of the 26.3 million people who live in Zaire, about 30,000 are European. The others are members of approximately 250 native African groups. Though the official language of Zaire is French, most Zaireans are Bantu-speaking peoples.

It is not actually known how the Bantu-speaking people arrived in Zaire. Some suspect that about the time of Christ, those from Cameroon and Nigeria, having learned farming techniques as far back as the Iron Age, grew strong, powerful and overpopulated. They needed more land in order to survive. As they traveled south, subtribes began to form and settle. It was not until they reached the Shaba region in southern Zaire, a grassy land much like the savannahs they had left behind, that they ended their migration and settled down to once again begin farming.

There are eighty-four groups of Bantu languages, and each group may contain as many as ten individual languages divided into hundreds of dialects spoken across central Africa. The Bantu dialects vary so much that people speaking one dialect cannot understand people speaking another. But the link to grouping them all into a blanket language called Bantu is based on the use of common prefixes and suffixes around a set of root words.

Lingala, which is spoken in central Zaire, is the country's traditional national language. It has incorporated so many French words into its vocabulary, that it has become the most important language in central Zaire, and is used by tradespeople on the Zaire River.

The most common Bantu language is Swahili. It is spoken

in much of East Africa and in the eastern portion of Zaire. Most documents and modern literature are now written in Swahili. Though there are fourteen dialects, Kingwana, or Congo Swahili, is spoken in Zaire and is the language used on radio broadcasts in the area.

The Bakongo is the largest group in Zaire, with a population of about four million. They live in western Zaire, in the Bas Zaire and Bandunda regions. Most are farmers whose main crops are bananas, cassava, maize, and sweet potatoes. Some grow coffee and cocoa for sale in markets.

The second largest group is the Baluba, a people who number about three million. Their dialects are Tshiluba in Kasai and Kiluba in Shaba, the two most populated Baluba areas.

The Baluba living in Kasai hastened to send their children to the schools that opened at the end of the last century. They also found jobs in the coppertowns once the railroads were opened. Before long, they controlled land along the rail lines. Others became teachers or white-collar workers.

The Balunda's main occupation in the seventeenth and eighteenth centuries was farming. A shortage of manpower to work the farms turned them into a militant group that captured Africans and made them slaves. They sold their own criminals into slavery.

Their power declined with the arrival of the Europeans in the mid-nineteenth century and through rivalry with neighboring groups.

South of the Zaire River between the Kasai and Sankuru rivers, live the Bakuba. The arrival of the Portuguese forced them to flee their original homeland in Gabon. At first, they settled near the Kwango River. But in the early part of the seventeenth century, warring tribes forced them further east to their present homelands.

The Bakuba are hunting and fishing people. They are also expert farmers. Traditionally, their clothing was made of bark-cloth and raffia. This raffia, even today, is used for weaving beautiful art objects and mats.

At first, the Bakuba were divided into small clans, each with its own leader. One of the chiefs, Shamba Bolongongo, became important in the history of these people. He built a strong army out of the many people who lived in his kingdom. He encouraged agriculture and introduced his people to corn and tomatoes—crops of the Portuguese. He taught them weaving and wood carving.

THE PYGMIES

Perhaps the most unusual people living in Equatorial Africa are the Pygmies. The largest concentration of Pygmies, the Mbuti, live on some 25,000 square miles (9,650 sq km) of rain forest along the banks of the Zaire River and its tributary, the Lualaba, and in the Ituri Forest in northeastern Zaire.

The Mbuti, who are hunters, continue to live in much the same way as they have for thousands of years. Pygmies ask little of life; they need only the basic minimums: food, shelter, and safety. Once they have hunted and gathered their necessities from the forest, they devote their day to visiting neighbors, playing with their children, and discussing family problems. Because of this simple, wholesome atttitude, Pygmy life is usually peaceful and secure.

The Pygmies live in close harmony with the land. These red-brown-skinned people, averaging 4 foot 6 inches (1.4 m) tall

*Isolated from the usual changes of time
and progress, this Pygmy relies on traditional drums
to communicate with people in nearby villages.*

at maturity, have retained their minimal Stone Age technological level. They have neither changed the land nor domesticated the animals. Though stone implements have been replaced by metal arrowheads and other more efficient tools have been given to them by other Bantu-speaking tribes, the Mbuti continue to pick mushrooms, fruit, nuts, and roots as the basis of their diet. They hunt for the meat they need and never take more than they use. As they deplete the available food in one particular area, they move onto another area and establish a camp there.

Ten or twelve families live in a camp. Each family lives in a beehive-shaped hut made of sticks and leaves. Many of the huts are set high up in trees so they cannot be reached by wild animals.

The family is a close-knit unit. Sometimes groups of families band together for hunting purposes. They begin as a large group and then break up into smaller groups. Men hang nets in bushes and stand guard with bows and arrows. Woman and children drive the game into the nets. Once the animals are killed, the hunters put them into baskets and bring them back to the village. Everyone shares the catch.

The future of the Pygmies is uncertain. During Belgium's control of Zaire, attempts were made to integrate the Pygmies into the Congo culture. At one time, the Congo government wanted the Pygmies to become more "civilized." They wanted to eliminate their poverty by teaching them how to farm. But the idea proved to be an error; Pygmies were unhappy living in villages. Many became ill and died. As a result, those remaining fled back into the forest, content to follow their own traditions. They had no need for the "modern" ways of life. Today, Zaire realizes that Pygmy tradition needs to be preserved, and that, rather than change the Pygmies, the government would do better to learn how the Pygmies have successfully thrived for so many years and how the government can support them so that their identity and way of life will not be lost.

RELIGION

It is estimated that half of Zaire's population is Roman Catholic, and perhaps another 25 percent is affiliated with other Christian churches. But people or groups who claim membership in a Christian religion may, and often do, share in the supernatural rituals of age-old African religions.

These religions all believe in one high god, the ultimate cause of everything. Often these high gods were ancestors of the chiefs or spirits of elements in nature.

Zairean societies believe there are spiritual powers in all things. Therefore, certain people or things seem to have the power to bring illness or some other condition on others. They are considered "witches" who have evil within them.

EDUCATION

Although education in Zaire is not required by law, it is considered important to the people.

After independence, Zaire found itself with few and poorly trained teachers and inadequate facilities. From 1968 through 1972, the government offered free primary and secondary education. As of 1972, education was no longer free, except for those who could not afford to pay.

The Ministry of Education was created to hire faculty and handle the planning and financing of the curriculum. It eliminated all religious and private schools.

After the Ministry became the Department of National Education, it began a program consisting of a six-year primary school course. This primary education prepared students for secondary school.

But there were still many problems: Rural areas did not receive the six-year program, and few students, even in cities, continued their education beyond the primary level. The curriculum offered poor preparation for the rural student. Primary school teachers were generally those who were not qualified to teach secondary schools.

Enrollment doubled and thereby caused a strain on the facilities. Problems arose: Teachers were generally foreigners; dropouts were many, and failure rates were high.

The government created agricultural and vocational schools in the hope of training young people to help raise the standard of living and the dwindling economy. But these two- to four-year programs did not offer adequate training.

On the higher education level, the National University of Zaire has three separate campuses. In 1976, there were over 25,000 students enrolled in the university.

As of 1973, the literacy rate in Zaire was only 30 percent, though there are 11,000 primary and secondary schools with a total enrollment of 3,627,223 students.

HEALTH CARE

The infant death rate in Zaire is extremely high. It is reported to be 104 for every 1,000 born. Much of this problem is caused by malnutrition and, in some cases, semistarvation due to poverty. In addition, the climate and humidity form a perfect breeding ground for insects which spread many tropical diseases, often worsened by poor diets and poor sanitation.

Many Zaireans in the rain forests live in crowded straw huts, making it easy for diseases to spread. A diet of bananas, cassavas, or beans cannot supply proper nutrition, and neither can meat which is always burned to the point that it has no nutritional value at all.

The tsetse fly is the common enemy. It transmits sleeping sickness through its bite. If treated early enough by antibiotics, the disease will not be serious. But with medical care so far away, often, little can be done to save the victim. In an attempt to stop the reproduction of the tsetse fly, many equatorial countries constantly spray insecticides from airplanes, or insist that vehicles and cattle pass through spraying sheds. But because the area is so large, these methods are generally ineffective.

Even more dangerous is the spread of malaria by mosquitoes. When possible, people are given quinine and stabrine which effectively prevent the disease. But, with so many people living so far apart and with transportation into the jungle so difficult, it is impossible to provide medicine for everyone.

THE ARTS

Zaire produces some of the most impressive statues, ivory carvings, and ebony sculptures in all Africa. But the artists never sign their names to their works. According to custom, they remain anonymous.

Their talent can be traced back to precolonial times when every hut was decorated with beautifully crafted carvings and mats. During colonialization, missionaries considered their statues and masks "heathen idols." They destroyed the works of art that existed and forbade any more from being made. By so doing, countless masterpieces were lost to the world.

Traditional Zairean music is vocal, but as in other African countries, the most widely used instrument is the drum. Originally the drum was used for sending messages, but later it became a rhythm instrument used for entertainment. Other traditional instruments are forms of the harp, zither, lute, horn, flute, whistle, and xylophone.

3

AROUND ZAIRE

KINSHASA

Until 1966, when many of the names in Zaire were changed from their British or French names to African names as part of a "return to authenticity" campaign, Kinshasa was known as Leopoldville. Like Brazzaville, 14 miles (22.53 km) across the Zaire River, it is a river-port center of commerce and government. It has a population of over two million.

Because it acts as a river terminal, manufacturing is a chief industry. Some factories process food, while others produce footwear, textiles, metalwork, and woodwork. Mills to refine imported wheat and turn it into food products are also located in the capital, as are breweries, motor vehicle-assembling parts, and cigarette-manufacturing plants.

KISANGANI

Located on the Lualaba River, where violent waterfalls inhibit navigation, Kisangani is the northeastern industrial center of Zaire —and as such, is also the site of factories for cigarette manufacturing, textile manufacturing, tire production, and metalworking.

LUBUMBASHI

Lubumbashi is also an industrial area. Once called Elizabethville, it is the main city in the copperbelt. Numerous railroad lines meet at Lubumbashi to carry raw materials such as cotton and synthetic fibers for fabric mills, and leather, plastic, and rubber for the footwear mills. It is also the site of an international airport and enjoys Africa's most pleasant climate.

THE MOUNTAINS

North of Lubumbashi are the Eastern Highlands, the highest and most rugged area of Zaire. They extend over 932 miles (1,500 km) north to Lake Mobutu Sese Seko. These mountains are sometimes 16,400 feet (5,000 m) high. East of this region is the Great Rift Valley. Because of the severe changes in altitude and its location straddling the equator, the vegetation is most unusual and varied.

Between Lake Mobutu Sese Seko (formerly Lake Albert) and Lake Idi Amin Dada (formerly Lake Edward), can be found the Ruwenzori Mountains, often called the Mountains of the Moon. So unusual is the foliage on these snowcapped mountains that common plants are sometimes as tall as trees. Their flowers, if they fall, are heavy enough to harm a passerby. Science has yet to unravel the mystery of their size. Leopards and elephants roam freely among the evergreens below the snow line. Above it, at an altitude of some 15,000 feet (4,500 m), dark brown bands ripple through the ice, the result of the dust of the dry seasons rising into the sky.

THE ECONOMY OF ZAIRE

Zaire is not an economically strong country. Two systems, "Zaire-anization" and "radicalization"—both designed to place foreign business in the hands of Zaire—have failed in recent years to solve the economic problems faced by the country. Basically, Zaire's trouble stems from the government's lack of true concern for finding an economic system that would help the people. Too much of Zaire's industry, farming, and mining was in the hands of the rich and politically strong. In addition, the collapse of copper and cobalt prices in 1974, the rise in oil prices, and basic world financial problems sent the once richest country in Africa into rapid decline.

There are other reasons: Zaire depended on Angola's Benguela Railway to transport its copper, cobalt, and manganese from Shaba. But the Angola civil war in 1977 shut down the railroad and forced Zaire to find other less-effective and more expensive routes. Food, as well, could not be transported, causing food prices to skyrocket. In addition, roads have not been cared for and natural resources have not been properly handled. President Mobutu's backing of expensive and elaborate new projects, such as a new dam and a steel mill, have taken priority over improving existing facilities. To make matters worse, there have been reports of embezzlement and graft in Mobutu's select group of political favorites.

This suspected government corruption, as well as runaway inflation, has caused soaring food prices. A loaf of bread now costs $1.75; a quart of milk, $6.00; and a dozen eggs, $12.00. But the average wage in Zaire is only $50.00 per month.

Zaire's economic future is uncertain, but there have been attempts to repair the damage. The European Economic Community and the World Bank will continue with financial aid, as will Belgium, Great Britain, Japan, West Germany, and the United States. But, repayment of the loan plus interest rates is and will be, a great burden.

AGRICULTURE
Because of the variety of climates and topography, Zaire can produce coffee, cocoa, rubber, oil palms, and sugar cane, as well as cotton, bananas, wheat, peanuts, and tea. Manioc (a root we call tapioca), maize, and rice are its major produce.

In the rich soil of the eastern highlands are grown many of the same fruits and vegetables grown in Europe and the United States: lettuce, cabbage, onions, beans, and peas. All these are raised on land passed on from one generation to the next.

FISH AND LIVESTOCK
Like so many of Zaire's other industries, the fishing industry has not met its potential. Fish can be found in all the lakes and rivers, but the annual catch declines each year because of the lack of concern by the government for fishing as a profit-making industry.

Fishermen use traps made of twigs and rope to catch fish in the Zaire River.

Livestock, thriving in the eastern highlands where the tsetse fly cannot live, is a major industry. Some livestock are raised for commercial markets, while others are raised on small, private ranches. On the increase is the production of sheep, goats, and hogs. The chickens, ducks, and their eggs are sold in Kinshasa markets.

MINING AND
METAL PRODUCTION

Minerals, such as copper, cobalt, zinc, manganese, gold, and silver, can be found in Shaba. The Kasai region produces diamonds and the Kivu area produces tin, tungsten, and gold. But with all these available ores, mining and production are on a rapid decline because of Zaire's financial difficulties. Money to finance mineral extraction is needed before the mines can show profits.

In 1977, Zaire began the "Mobutu Plan," a three-year program for the reorganization of transportation, the redevelopment of agriculture, and the reutilization of mines. Zaire is assured of aid from friendly countries and private sources to help bail it out of its financial woes.

GABON AND ITS PEOPLE

Gabon is rather a small country with an area of 160,200 square miles (267,000 sq km), and a population of just over one million. It is bordered by the Atlantic Ocean on the west and the People's Republic of the Congo on the south and east. Equatorial Guinea, Cameroon, and the Central African Republic are at its northern border.

Gabon has two rainy seasons. From January through May is the first, and the second begins slowly in October and reaches its full strength in January. From May to September, weather is generally drier.

Gabon's west coast is a sandy strip on the Atlantic. In places, it is 125 miles (201 km) wide, fringed with bays, lagoons, and mouths of rivers emptying into the ocean. Inland of this coastal strip lies a 1,969 foot- (600 cm) high plateau covered with grassy savannahs and dense forests. The Ngoumie and Okano rivers cut through the forests.

THE PEOPLE

Though the official language of Gabon is French, most Gabonese are Bantu-speaking people. The Gabonese are descendants of many ethnic groups that came from all parts of Africa during the past seven hundred years.

About one fourth of Gabon's population are the Bantu-speaking Fang people. They were originally from northern Cameroon, but were driven out about two hundred years ago. Many now live in the Ogooue River basin. Most Fangs favor trade as a livelihood. Still others have joined the timber industry, moving from one lumber camp to another. However, in northern Gabon, others have become farmers and cocoa-growers.

Other Bantu-speaking tribes, such as the Eshira, the Bapounou, the Bateke, and the Okande make up most of the remaining ethnic population. Many immigrants now inhabit Gabon because of the extensive industry on the coast. Most are from other French-speaking African nations, but there are also about 50,000 Europeans—the majority French.

THE PYGMIES

Besides Bantu-speaking peoples, Gabon is inhabited by Pygmies. Anthropologists believe they are one of the oldest races on earth, and certainly the oldest in Gabon. A Bantu legend explains that when the first people arrived on earth, the Pygmies were already here. An Egyptian papyrus records that in 2500 B.C., a pharaoh sent men into the African interior to bring back dwarfs to entertain him—much like court jesters would.

Pygmies are an independent group living not only in Gabon, but in the forests that stretch from the Atlantic Ocean straight across Africa to the lakes east of Zaire.

POPULATION DIVISIONS

The geographical division of Gabon's people is odd indeed. Libreville, the capital, has 250,000 people. However, the population is close to zero in the areas of the Mayumba Mountains, the Les Aberilles region, the Middle Ogooue valley, and the Crystal Mountains. On the other hand, in the north, at Woleri N'Tem, live the greatest number of people. But even in this densely populated area, there are zones in which no one lives. Some feel it is because diseases may have chased people from their homes. Others feel that conflict among the fifty ethnic groups caused many people to move.

Whatever the reason, these fifty ethnic groups speak over forty different dialects, many similar to each other. The relationship of one group to the other is based on various factors: some live in the same area; some are joined by similar customs and laws; some have been conquered by the same enemy; and some are joined together out of necessity. However, they all share many common legends of their origin.

RELIGION

These legends are part of the Gabonese people's age-old religions, religions they continue to follow, though today about 260,000 Gabonese are Christians and 3,000 are Muslims.

African religions include a belief in magic and even in psychic powers. Modern life is destroying these beliefs. But there are those who are working to preserve many of the traditions so that the Gabonese can retain their age-old culture.

EDUCATION

Though primary school attendance is 100 percent in Gabon, the literacy rate remains at only 30 percent. There are not enough qualified teachers, nor are there proper schools for the children. Gabon has 734 primary and secondary schools, not nearly enough for the population.

An additional problem is the variety of languages in Gabon and the other Bantu countries. In which language are lessons taught? In which language are the books printed? Until a choice is made, teaching programs and methods will remain inadequate.

Founded in 1970, the University of Libreville offers courses in the humanities, letters, law, economics, and the sciences. It includes a library, faculty housing, and a medical school. Future plans include additional library facilities, a language laboratory, and student housing.

Adults, too, must be educated. Training schools in rural areas to teach health, nutrition, and new agricultural methods are open to both men and women. Literacy classes for adults continue to expand. At present, there are 500 in the interior areas.

HEALTH

Like the other equatorial countries, Gabon is plagued by malaria, sleeping sickness, malnutrition, and a skin ulcer known as yaws. Much-needed hospital facilities are not yet available, especially in the interior of the country. There are approximately 98 people for every available hospital bed and 5,000 people for every doctor. Eighty-three out of every 1,000 children die at birth. Proper sanitation and disease prevention methods are also lacking, especially in rural areas.

Gabon realizes it has poor health facilities and plans to correct them by building a hospital in every provincial capital, a dispensary in every large town, a clinic in every main village area, and rural health care centers in outlying regions. The training of nurses, the reduction of infant deaths, and instruction in basic hygiene techniques is also a priority for the near future.

THE ARTS

Art in Gabon is different in meaning from art in other parts of the world. Gabonese artists do not intentionally create beauty. They are only creating a way of fighting the evil forces in the universe. If their creation has artistic value, it is of no importance to the creators. It is for this reason that as missionaries converted more Gabonese to Christianity, many artists willingly gave up making their masks and statues. They had no need for them if they were not to continue the ancient religious ceremonies. Beautiful works of art were therefore lost forever.

Many statues represented the spirits of ancestors. On special occasions they were anointed with palm oil or animal blood. Often, boxes containing ancestral bones were kept and were surrounded by statues.

Masks are even more plentiful than statues. Often, these masks, carved of soft wood and adorned with raffia, feathers, mirrors, or antlers, represented the spirit of the dead. They were sometimes worn by those who were being initiated into mystic religious groups.

Music is part of the life of the Gabonese. It is heard in their religious ceremonies, while they are involved in their daily work, while they are at home, or at festivals.

Aside from the drum, the *ngombi,* a seven-string harp or zither, is the most typical instrument. It is made of vanilla bean root and plucked with the thumb and index finger. A wooden sounding box holds a crosspiece for the strings. Other commonly used instruments are rattles, bells, tambourines, and the human voice.

Originally part of religious rituals, dances are also performed for entertainment. In this way, they are being preserved.

It is feared, however, that, as a result of modernization, these dances will be forgotten as new generations lose interest in native religions.

6

AROUND GABON

LIBREVILLE

Until the arrival of President Bongo, Libreville, though the capital of Gabon, remained a sleepy little town of earth-paved streets, one-story wooden houses and straw-walled or corrugated metal-roofed huts. Today, it shows a startling rebirth.

The new Libreville is rapidly becoming a city of wider streets and boulevards, expensive hotels, restaurants, night clubs, and discos. Modern markets, new and enlarged schools, post offices, and movie theaters are being built.

But this overnight transformation has its drawbacks. Recent "renovations," a catchword coined by Bongo for all of Gabon, have turned Libreville into a jigsaw puzzle. Nothing seems to fit. Streets have been moved and shops have suddenly disappeared. Government offices are scattered about so that nonresidents of the town cannot find them.

Down near the sea life is a little calmer. The traffic moves slowly but steadily. People stroll by the beautiful residences on tree-lined streets.

PORT GENTIL

Located on an island off the coast, Port Gentil (with a population of 70,000), can only be reached by air or by sea. Gabon's industrial and commercial center, it is the home of refineries and the world's largest wood-veneer factory.

Port Gentil has a nearly timeless charm. The town is covered with flowering trees of all shapes and sizes. In addition, it has an interesting blend of architecture. Modern buildings are found on the main streets, but elsewhere, styles of centuries gone by can be seen.

LAMBARENE

About 154 miles (246 km) from Libreville is Lambarene, an island in the Ogooue River, once only reached by ferry, but now joined to the mainland by two bridges. Lambarene is best known for Dr. Albert Schweitzer's mission hospital.

Albert Schweitzer was born in 1875 in Alsace-Lorraine. When he was thirty-one, Schweitzer enrolled in medical school. In 1913, after eight years of medical studies, he chose the hottest, wettest, and most disease-ridden spot in the world for him and his new wife to build a hospital—on the Ogooue River in Gabon, 50 miles (80.46 km) south of the equator.

Within a few years, the hospital became a medical community—a group of buildings for patients, some of whom traveled days to get the care they needed. It is this care that made Dr.

Apartment complexes and multi-storied buildings make Libreville, the capital of Gabon, a very modern city.

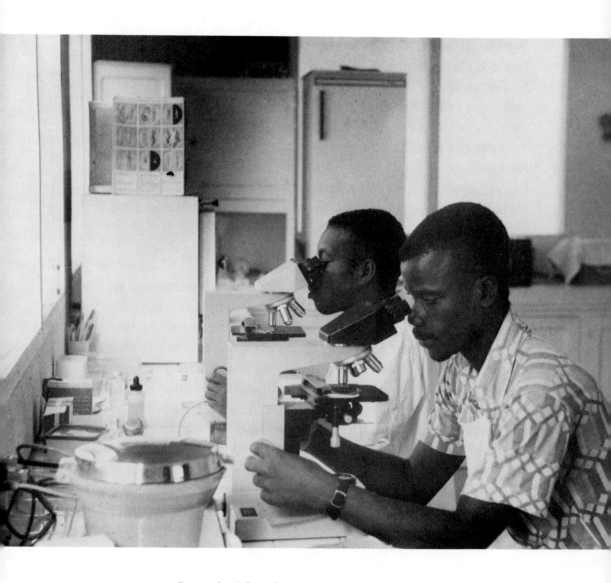

*Started with only the most primitive facilities,
the hospital Albert Schweitzer founded in 1913 now boasts
of several buildings and modern medical equipment.*

Schweitzer so important to Africa and to the world. Patients were permitted to bring their families to stay with them. Family members helped with chores in and around the hospital. Patients who were well enough helped out too. Other than this work, no other payment was ever necessary.

Aside from an electrically equipped operating room, the rest of Dr. Schweitzer's hospital was simple. Oil lamps were used, beds were wooden, and animals roamed around freely. Patients were never turned away, and treatment for any disease was given with gentleness, generosity, and cleanliness.

After World War II, people around the world began to hear about Dr. Schweitzer's noble efforts. In 1952, he was honored with the Nobel Peace Prize. Dr. Schweitzer took the forty thousand dollars in prize money and bought supplies to repair an adjoining leper colony he had built.

Albert Schweitzer died in Lambarene in 1965 at age ninety. His hospital is still in use, although a new modern one has since replaced it.

7
THE ECONOMY OF GABON

Due to inflation, inadequate transportation, and an imbalance of revenue sources, Gabon, like its neighbor, the Republic of the Congo, is beset with financial problems. Though Gabon's industries show a profit, its national debt continues to rise. Not until the Transgabon Railroad, built to transport ore from mines to refineries to ports, is completed, will Gabon be able to get on its feet. But, with a lack of capital and rising prices, the progress of the railroad's completion is slower than expected.

To bolster its economy, Gabon has been encouraging foreign investments from private companies in the United States, France, Germany, Italy, Japan, and South Korea. It believes in a system of free enterprise, and therefore has not exerted government control over business or industry.

AGRICULTURE AND LIVESTOCK
Though more than 80 percent of Gabon's population make a living from agriculture, until recently, the growth of crops for either personal use or export was a low priority. But, under the new "Third National Development Plan," agriculture will be considered more important.

Gabon's farmers grow bananas, plantains, rice, cassavas (manioc or tapioca), corn, as well as the more common fruits and garden vegetables. Export crops include coffee, cocoa, peanuts, palm oil, copra, sugar, and rubber. But these exports are limited.

Livestock production in Gabon is conducted by only two companies. Also raised are goats, sheep, pigs, and poultry. Until Gabon is able to raise enough livestock for its population, it will continue to import meat and meat products.

INDUSTRY

Much of Gabon's revenue comes from its oil production. It is currently in an oil boom that the government hopes will continue through 1992. Some fifty million dollars is being spent to explore both inland and offshore oil possibilities. There are currently fourteen companies producing crude oil in Gabon. Their economic future looks bright—for the time being.

Gabon is the world's largest exporter of manganese, its second-ranking natural resource, after oil. The Moanda reserves produce more manganese than any other quarry outside of those in the Soviet Union.

Another important resource is uranium, sold extensively to the United States, France, Sweden, and Japan. In addition, Gabon produces an abundance of iron ore and gold.

Nearly half of Gabon's manufacturing output comes from ore refineries in Pointe-Clarette. Other plants produce cement, textiles, shoes, soap, cigarettes, paint, beer, flour, and sugar.

TRANSPORTATION

When the 600-mile (96,000-km) Transgabon Railroad is completed in a few years, Gabon will be able to link the port cities of

Owanda and Santa Clara with Franceville, to speed up the transport of manganese. It will also connect the cities of Booue and Belinga, for the rapid movement of iron ore. The new railroad will pass through the forest and swamplands and over the major rivers. It is the hope of Gabon's future, "the priority of priorities," as President Bongo has said.

Along with the development of the railroad, roads will be paved, air service will be expanded, and deep water ports at Port-Gentil will be established for improved cargo service.

It is hoped that these developments will offset Gabon's financial difficulties so that it will soon become a self-sustaining nation.

8

THE CONGO
AND ITS PEOPLE

The People's Republic of the Congo is a narrow strip of land whose area is 132,000 square miles (342,000 sq km) and whose population is 1,420,000. The Central African Republic and Cameroon are its northern neighbors, while Gabon is on its west. Zaire, separated by the Congo (Zaire) and Ubangi rivers, borders it on the east and south. The small tip of Angola, called Cabinda, also touches its southern border. The Congo has a small Atlantic coastline.

The climate in most of the Congo is hot and humid. Its temperature ranges between 73° F–80° F (21° C–27° C). From May to September is the dry season and in October the short rainy season begins. The rain subsides for about a month, from mid-December until mid-January, and then a long rainy season begins and continues until May.

The Republic of the Congo is divided into four natural areas. The Coastal Plain runs along the South Atlantic Coast. It stops at the foothills of the Crystal Mountains. The South-Central region is covered by the fertile Niari Valley. The Central Highlands are basically plateaus and hilly plains. The largest area is the Congo River Basin, situated in the northeast. Dense rain forests and swampland cover the lower regions while dry savannahs are found in the upper areas.

THE PEOPLE

There are four main Congo ethnic groups, all of which are Bantu-speaking:

The Bakongo, said to be the most advanced people in Western Equatorial Africa, make up 45 percent of the population. Most of the Bakongo are farmers who grow cassava, maize, yams, and bananas. They live around Brazzaville in small villages controlled by their local leaders whose rule has been handed down through the years.

The Bateke, who number about 80,000 (20 percent of the population), came from the northwest and settled on the plateau north of Brazzaville which bears their name. Historically, they were hunters, warriors, copper miners, and slave traders, who lost their strength when the French and Belgians began to build commercial empires.

The Bobangi (also called the Mboshi) live in the Congo basin and Likouala regions. Of the 80,000 Bobangi, most earn a living by fishing or trading, though some practice agriculture. The Likouala, a subgroup of the Bobangi, live on the banks of the Congo. Their villages are built on high ground to protect them from floods. Because fishing is their main occupation, each family is given fishing rights to a certain section of the river. These rights are passed down from one generation to the next.

The Sangha, whose population is about 30,000, also live in the Likouala region of the northeast Congo, a wet forest area between the Sangha and Ubangi rivers. Though little is known about the Sangha, it is thought that they came into the area about two hundred years ago, accompanied by the Babinga Pygmies. The Pygmies still trade their game for Sangha agriculture products.

Besides being the homeland of Bantu-speaking people, the northern portion of the Congo is inhabited by the Sudanese, who migrated from North Africa. There are also about 10,000 non-Africans, most of whom are French. French remains the Congo's official language.

Three quarters of the citizens of the Congo live in the south. About one third of the total population is spread among the four major cities: Brazzaville, the capital, Pointe-Noire, Jacob, and Loubomo.

THE FAMILY

The need for better jobs and education has forced many young people to move into larger urban centers. This migration has caused a change in the traditional family structure. However, in the rural areas traditions, though modified, are still observed.

The traditional family structure is based on "lineage," that is, how one generation is descended from another. This structure is held together by strong social and religious values which are used to train children to respect their elders, and to develop proper behavior, attitudes, and religious principles.

The life-style in the cities is becoming more and more "westernized." As a result, the extended family, of necessity, has been left behind.

Most wage earners live and work in Brazzaville and Pointe-Noire, where salaries are higher than in rural villages. But these workers are unaccustomed to the responsibilities of working at city jobs. Therefore, unemployment is high. And, along with unemployment, comes poverty.

RELIGION
Even though most Congolese are Christians, nearly half of the population continues to practice some sort of ancient traditional religion.

The Bakongo believe that the world began in darkness while the earth was covered by water. This world was ruled by the god, Nzambi. One day, he became ill and spit out the sun, the moon, and the stars. Later, he spit out the animals and humans. It is this kind of myth that joins the traditional beliefs with organized religion.

HEALTH
The Congolese, like most people living in neighboring hot, humid nations, suffer a high rate of lung disease. Yellow fever, smallpox, and leprosy also afflict many of the people. To make matters worse, malnutrition, water pollution, and disease-carrying insects and rodents create additional health problems.

Small villages do not have sewerage systems or proper waste disposal methods. Contagious diseases are often spread through insects which hover around shallow water wells, poorly ventilated huts, and open pit latrines.

Because so much of the Congo's food must be imported and because imported food is so expensive, diets are not well-balanced. Therefore, nutrition comes from a diet of manioc (cassava), plantains, bananas, rice, sugar, corn, and sweet potatoes—generally starchy, high-calorie foods. In some areas where fruit is grown, the diet is supplemented by pineapples and citrus

[48]

fruits. However, fresh meat is hardly eaten, especially in the poorer rural sections. Fish is usually exported and so it is rarely eaten by the fishing communities. A lack of fresh meat and fish causes a deficiency of important nutrients in the Congolese diet.

Finally, refrigeration and storage are totally inadequate—so foods, subjected to the hot, humid climate, spoil easily.

Though health and medical services, provided by the government and the United Nations, have been expanded in the last ten years, they still do not meet all the needs of the people.

The Congo suffers from a lack of trained medical personnel. With the help of the United Nations and France, technical help is on the increase. It is hoped that with more medical aid, major health problems can be treated more effectively and efficiently in the future.

EDUCATION

For centuries, communication in the Congo has been through the use of the "talking drum." Certain elders, all of whom were men, would pass on important information through a series of drum signals that only they could play and understand. Though the drum is still in use, radio, TV, the telephone, three daily newspapers, and formal education have minimized the drum's importance.

Free and compulsory education for all children between the ages of six and sixteen was begun in 1970. Under the supervision of the Ministry of Information, Education and Cultural Affairs, over 90 percent (400,000) of all school-age children attend more than 1,000 primary and secondary schools. Rural schools stress agriculture, manual skills, or other forms of instruction for the pupil's working life. Urban schools follow a

*Although children in the Congo are required to attend
school until they are sixteen years old, only about
one out of five is able to read and write.*

similar curriculum, but agriculture is not taught. However, the literacy rate is only 20 percent.

Higher education is administered by the Federation of Equatorial Africa—a joint effort of the Congo, the Central African Republic, Gabon, and Chad. Degrees in law, science, the humanities, and education are offered in the Congo University. However, qualified students may attend a university in one of the other countries if they wish degrees in other subjects. Today, attempts are being made to raise the low literacy rate, to develop more worthwhile curricula and to upgrade teacher training programs.

THE ARTS

The arts and crafts of the Congo traditionally consisted of ceremonial masks, statues, and religious objects. Much of the work was not realistic, but took on a mysterious quality. Most common were interpretations of the human head and the animal forms.

Painting is usually for religious ceremonial objects or for textiles. Some beautiful, if temporary, painting is also done on the human body as part of religious ceremonies. Weaving, basketry, pottery making, and ironworking are also popular art forms.

In the mid-1960s, many artists stopped carving religious articles and began mass-producing masks and statues for sale to tourists. As a result, much of the beauty and originality of these works of art was lost. Therefore, the government created the Directorate of Culture to insure that Congolese tradition and art history would not disappear.

Daily life, religious ceremonies, and special family events

all include music and dance. It is as much a part of the Congolese people as their heartbeats.

The Congolese people sing to relieve the boredom of hard work, or to make the work seem easier. There are songs about women, pounding grain or hoeing a garden, men going hunting or fishing, boatmen paddling canoes, youngsters being initiated into religious cults, and medicine men blessing their magic potions. Like the songs and dances, the style of musical instruments is also varied. Drums are the most popular instruments. They are usually made entirely of wood, or of wood with a skin stretched tightly on the playing surface.

The *sanzi,* a very small piano-style instrument, is popular in the Congo. It has a hollow wooden base to which metal or reed strips are attached. The free ends of the strips are plucked with the thumbs. In addition, rattles, flutes, whistles, and now, the guitar, are played throughout the country.

9
AROUND THE CONGO

BRAZZAVILLE

Brazzaville, the capital city of the Congo, is in the south, 14 miles (22.53 km) directly across the Congo (Zaire) River from Kinshasa, Zaire's capital. It has a population of about 300,000.

A modern, thriving urban center since 1945, Brazzaville is the terminal city of the 500-mile (800-km) Ocean Railroad that begins at Pointe-Noire. Brazzaville has developed into a major city since the completion of the railroad's construction in 1934. People from the northern forest lands and from the river borders came to find work and a new way of life. Many have been unsuccessful and this feeling of frustration has only added to the rivalry of tribespeople who now live side by side in the city.

Brazzaville's river-port serves as the terminal of all commerce on the Congo's 4,000 miles (6,400 km) of navigable streams and rivers. It is here that goods and passengers arriving in Brazzaville can ferry to Kinshasa or go by rail to Pointe-Noire. In recent years, the port has been expanded to

*Women march in Brazzaville on the anniversary
of the 1963 revolution in which the
French-supported government was overturned.*

meet an increase in the amount of goods that may develop in the future.

The main branch of the Congo's 5,100 mile (8,160 km) highway system links Brazzaville west to Pointe-Noire and north to Oresso. Because of the tropical climate and rugged terrain, these highways were in poor condition. In 1969, an internal road repair project was begun to resurface the main route with asphalt.

Because of these available transportation facilities, Brazzaville is also the home of many manufacturing and processing plants. Among these are a sugar refinery, a soap factory, a soft drink plant, a brewery and malt house, a textile company, a book factory, and a phonograph record company—either financed by other governments or with Congolese capital.

POINTE-NOIRE
In addition to being the railroad and main highway link to Brazzaville, Pointe-Noire is the Congo's only actual seaport. Though it is one of the best equipped ports in West and Central Africa, it is not a natural port and must be protected by dikes. It is a modern, well-maintained facility capable of handling the output of potash mines. It is also a berth for ore ships and oil tankers.

Pointe-Noire maintains a modern jet international airport to transport goods and passengers to cities in Africa and other countries. And like Brazzaville, it is the home of many manufacturing and processing plants. A brewery, a soft drink plant, a shoe and sandal factory, and a glassworks are all helping to eliminate the Congo's national debt.

WILDLIFE PRESERVES

The Congo's two main reserves—Lefini and Divenie—are not the foremost in the equatorial area. However, their savannahs (grasslands) are havens for elephants, buffalo, and hippos. Chimpanzees and gorillas, as well as colorful parrots and butterflies, can be found in their forestlands.

10
THE ECONOMY OF THE CONGO

Like so many other nations, the Congo's major economic problems are unemployment, underdevelopment of land and resources, and a low standard of living.

To survive, the Congo depends heavily upon imports. Since 1963, it has made several trade agreements with the People's Republic of China, the Soviet Union, and the other Communist countries to import products for its people. With the help of the French government, modern farming techniques were introduced. Agricultural settlements were developed so that farmers could cultivate parcels of land given to them by the government.

Aside from farming for self-use, which is still the majority of the population's source of income, commercial farming was begun. Ground was cleared and crops were rotated to preserve the soil's nutrients. Yams, peanuts, taros, maize, gourds, and peas were grown in addition to common garden vegetables. When the land could no longer produce a healthy crop, it was abandoned for about ten years and crops were then planted somewhere else. Except near large cities, land in the Congo is never scarce.

European companies brought in heavy equipment to cultivate the land. These companies also sold crops for the farmers.
But government-sponsored farms, begun in order to develop
modern farming methods and to research expanding crop development, were not successful. Instead, cooperative villages have
been instituted to help the farmer get crops to the market, establish credit, and buy machinery.

Sugar and tobacco are the largest cash (export) crops. But
coffee, cocoa, bananas, rice, and peanuts are also grown for
commercial use, though rarely for export.

FORESTRY AND
ANIMAL HUSBANDRY

Until the discovery of oil in 1968 and an oil boom in 1974, timber accounted for more than half of the Congo's exports. Poor
transportation makes it difficult to remove the timber, but when
it can be floated downstream, great profits can be derived from
the forest.

Limba and okoume (a mahogany) are the principle woods
grown, but *tchifola* and *acajou* are also grown. All these trees are
felled as part of forest research projects. They are inventoried,
and once chopped down, are replanted. In addition, trees that
grow quickly are planted to create new forestlands.

Until a breed of cattle was developed in Zaire that could
combat the disease carried by the tsetse fly, cattle production in
the Congo was limited.

Government-owned ranches and breeding enterprises run
by private companies have increased meat and milk production,
but not to the extent the Congo hopes to reach. Nevertheless, cattle, sheep, goats, and pigs continue to be raised. Poultry and eggs,

because they are not popular Congolese foods, serve as prime exports. Ninety percent of meat eaten by the Congolese is imported.

FISHING
Fishing zones have been claimed for centuries by various ethnic groups living along the rivers. Fish are usually caught by nets, though some people fish from canoes or from small motorboats.

European companies control most of the sea-fishing. However, some local people do make a small-scale living from it. The major fish caught are bass, pink and gray dorado, sole, and sardines—most of which are sold in Brazzaville, Pointe-Noire, Dolisie, and Jacob. Fish-processing has become a growing industry.

MANUFACTURING
There is really no heavy industry in the Congo, but new industrial plants continue to be built to process by-products of existing industries.

Food-processing is dominated by sugar refineries, peanut processors, and palm oil mills. The great mills of the Congo refine wheat that is imported from France. Flour from maize, rice, and manioc, as well as cattlefeed, are also produced.

Tonic and quinine water, cola, lemon, orange, and grenadine drinks are processed. The production of palm wine, an inexpensive substitute for red wine, is also a thriving business. In addition, fabrics, leather shoes, and plastic and rubber sandals are manufactured.

Because of the size of the timber industry, wood-processing plants are important to the Congo economy. New railroads, though still in insufficient numbers, transport timber to sawmills that are mostly owned by European companies. Other wood is made into veneers, crates, barrels, furniture, and even stick matches. In addition, soap, beer, cement, and cigarettes are produced.

MINING

While prospecting for ore in 1959, miners discovered large deposits of high-grade potash at Gare Holle, near Pointe-Noire. These deposits are among the largest and richest in the world. Other mined minerals are iron, tin, zinc, limestone, copper, lead, gold, and diamonds. But these ores are extracted in small quantities and are not part of the Congo's economic strength.

Oil production remains low, but greater development is planned, especially in offshore oil production.

11

AFTERWORD

The Equatorial countries of Africa have undergone extensive change during the past five hundred years. From primitive tribal lands, to oppressed territories, to free and independent nations, they have suffered from ignorance, slavery, poverty, and misunderstanding. Yet, they have survived. And from all appearances, they will continue to grow and prosper.

During the past few years, Gabon has become the world's largest exporter of manganese, a member of OPEC, and a nonpermanent member of the United Nations Security Council. In the future, its mineral resources will provide substantial income for its people. Today, Port Gentil is undergoing great industrial development. Libreville and Franceville are about to follow. As Gabon becomes less an agricultural nation, more of its people will be moving from underdeveloped villages into modern cities to attempt a new life.

Like the future of Gabon, the future of the Congo will depend on its mineral wealth. France continues to be the Congo's chief partner. It has provided financial aid through its companies that now control much of the Congo's commerce and industry. France recently opened new mines and boosted the extraction and export of potash which has become the country's largest business.

Other important exports include diamonds smuggled from Zaire, timber and agricultural products, phosphates, and most recently, offshore oil.

Pointe-Noire has become a mining center, as well as a manufacturing center. Small villages will follow in its footsteps as they too are converted into bustling industrial complexes.

Zaire's strength will come from its hydroelectric projects like those near Kinshasa. With new power to run industrial plants, it will boost its production of cement, textiles, and steel.

These equatorial countries, once known for their mysterious, dense rain forests where savage animals and strange natives lived, are now known as countries that have joined the many industrial nations around the globe as contributors to the greater good of humanity.

FOR FURTHER READING

Addison, John. *Ancient Africa*. New York: John Day, 1970.

Bleeker, Sonia. *The Pygmies, Africans of the Congo Forest*. New York: William Morrow, 1968.

The Encyclopedia of Africa. New York: Franklin Watts, 1976.

Hall-Quest, Olga W. *With Stanley in Africa*. New York: E. P. Dutton, 1961.

Hall, Richard. *Discovery of Africa*. New York: Grosset & Dunlap, 1970.

Joseph, Joan. *Black African Empires*. New York: Franklin Watts, 1974.

McKown, Robin. *The Colonial Conquest of Africa*. New York: Franklin Watts, 1971.

———. *The Republic of Zaire*. New York: Franklin Watts, 1972.

Murphy, E. Jefferson. *Understanding Africa*. New York: Thomas Y. Crowell, 1978.

Turnbull, Colin. *The People of Africa*. Cleveland, Ohio: World Publishing, 1962.

INDEX

"Mobutu Plan," 30
Mokako, 4
Music
    in the Congo, 52
    in Gabon, 35
    in Zaire, 24
Muslims, 33

Ngouabi, Marien, 13, 14

Ocean Railroad, 53

Pointe-Noire, Congo, 47, 55, 62
Port Gentil, Gabon, 39, 61
Portugal, 2
Pygmies
    of Gabon, 32
    of Zaire, 18–21

Religion
    in the Congo, 48
    in Gabon, 33
    in Zaire, 21
Roman Catholicism, 21
Ruwenzori Mountains, 26

Sangha, 46–47
Sassou-Ngouesso, Denis, 14
Schweitzer, Albert, 39–40
Sculpture
    in the Congo, 52

    in Gabon, 35
    in Zaire, 23
Simbas, 11
Stanley, Henry M., 4
Swahili, 16–17

Transgabon Railroad, 42, 43–44

Vivi, Congo, 4

Woleri N'Tem, Gabon, 33
World War I, 6–7
World War II, 7–8

Yhombi-Opango, Joachim, 14
Youlou, Fulbert, 12–13

Zaire, 1
    the arts in, 23–24
    borders of, 15
    climate of, 15
    economy of, 27–30
    education in, 21–22
    future of, 62
    geography of, 15, 25–26
    health in, 22–23
    history of, 10–12
    peoples of, 15–21
    religion in, 21
Zaire, National University of, 22